Origins of Christianity

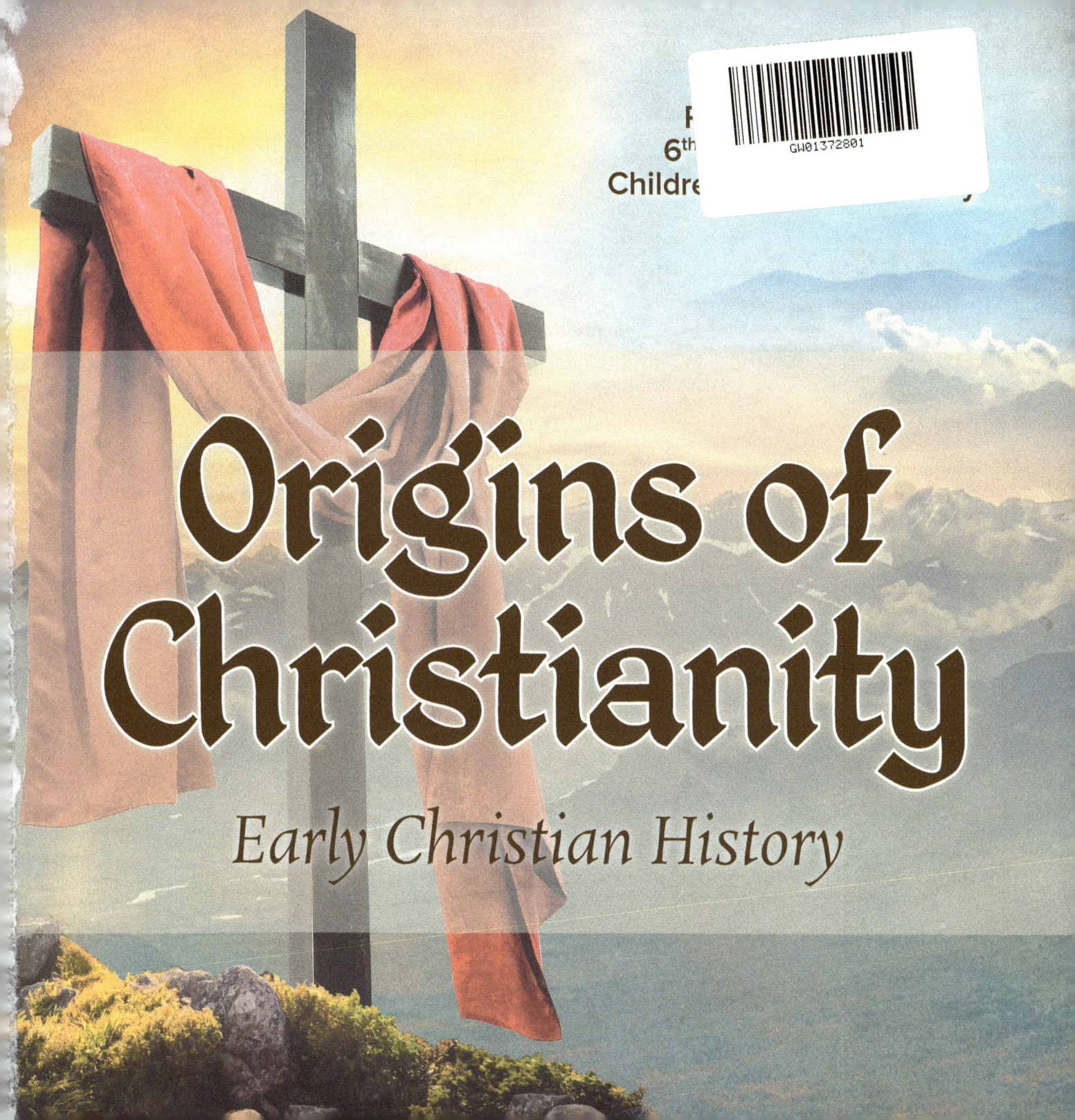

Early Christian History

ONE TRUE FAITH
RELIGION & SPIRITUALITY

First Edition, 2020

Published in the United States by Speedy Publishing LLC, 40 E Main Street, Newark, Delaware 19711 USA.

© 2020 One True Faith Books, an imprint of Speedy Publishing LLC

All rights reserved.

Without limiting the rights under the copyright reserved above, no part of this publication may be reproduced, stored in or introduced into a retrieval system, or transmitted, in any form, or by any means (electronic, mechanical, photocopying, recording, or otherwise), without the prior written permission of the copyright owner.

All images in this book have been reproduced with the knowledge and prior consent of the artists concerned, and no responsibility is accepted by producer, publisher, or printer for any infringement of copyright or otherwise arising from the contents of this publication.

One True Faith Books are available at special discounts when purchased in bulk for industrial and sales-promotional use. For details contact our Special Sales Team at Speedy Publishing LLC, 40 E Main Street, Newark, Delaware 19711 USA. Telephone (888) 248-4521 Fax: (210) 519-4043.

10 9 8 7 6 * 5 4 3 2 1

Print Edition: 9781541950535
Digital Edition: 9781541952331

See the world in pictures. Build your knowledge in style.
www.speedypublishing.com

Contents

What is Christianity? 5

The New Testament 11

The Early Life of Jesus Christ 17

Jesus Went to His Father's House 27

Jesus Performed Miracles 35

Jesus Taught by Telling Parables 43

Jesus Dies on the Cross 49

The Apostles Spread the Word 57

Paul Travels Throughout the Mediterranean 63

The Romans Persecuted the Christians 71

Summary 77

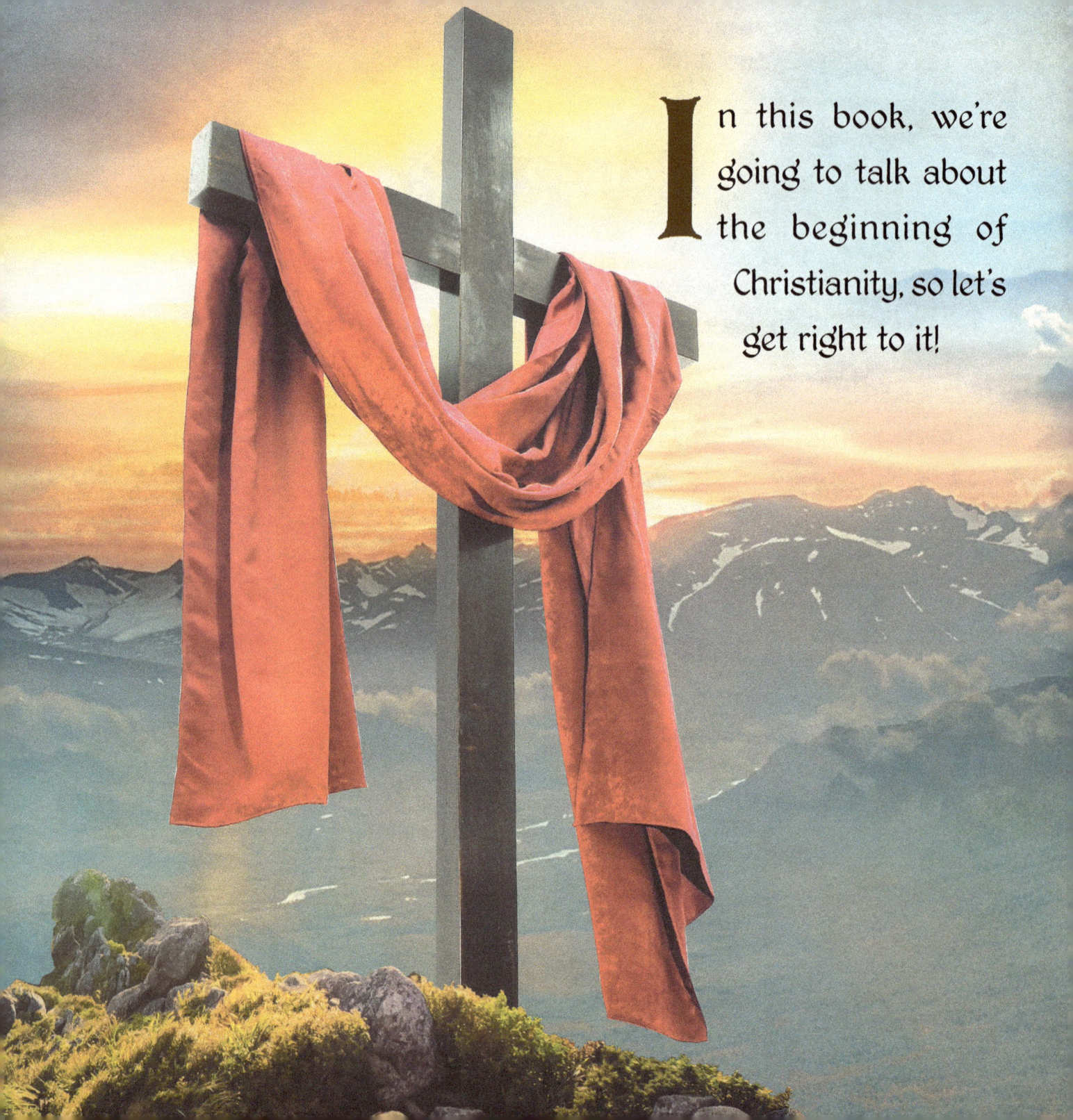

In this book, we're going to talk about the beginning of Christianity, so let's get right to it!

What is Christianity?

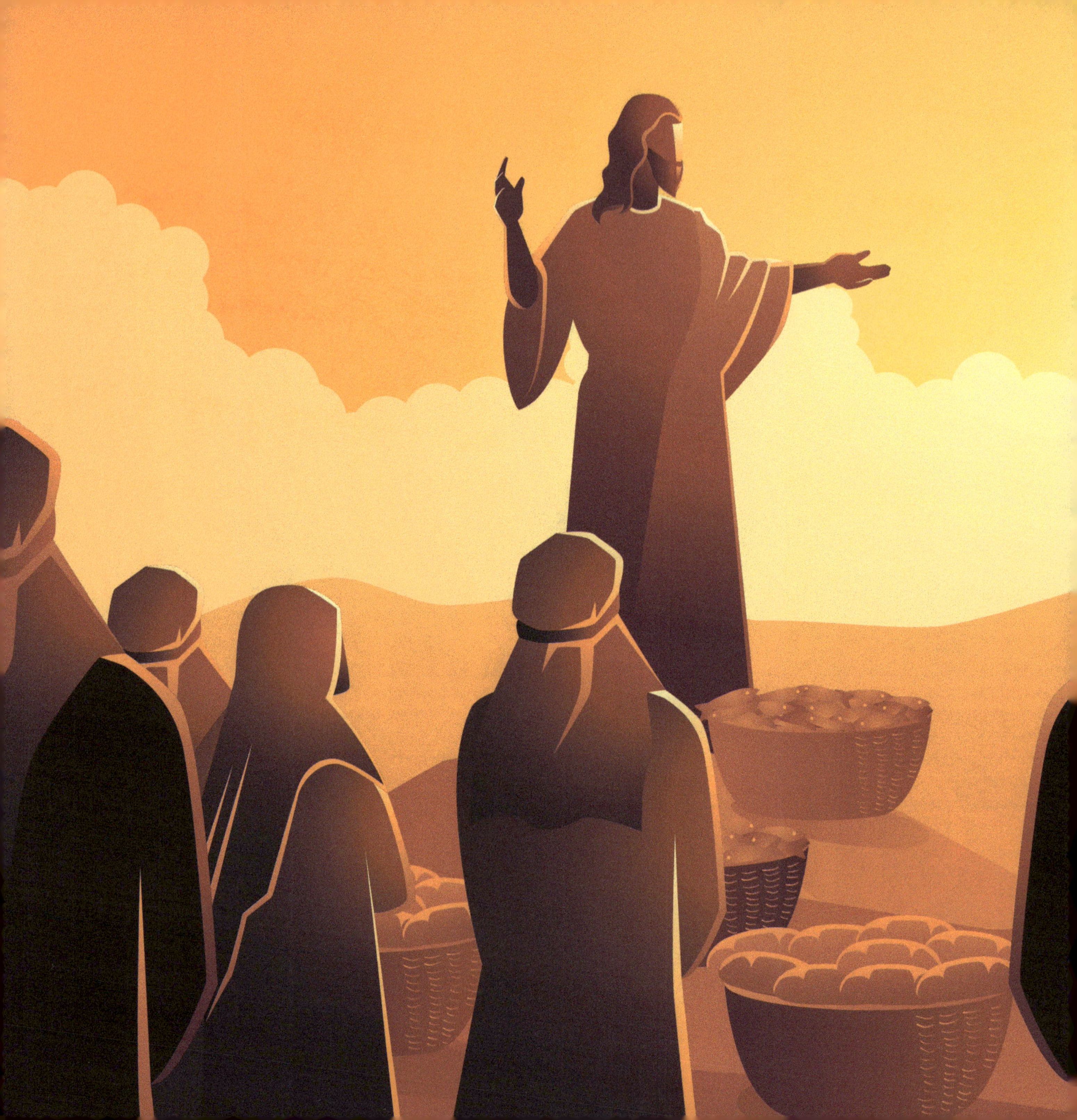

Christianity is a religion based on the belief that Jesus Christ is the Son of God. The first Christians were Roman Catholics. Then, the Eastern Orthodox Catholics split from the Roman Catholics.

The first Christians were Roman Catholics.

During the time of the Reformation, Protestants separated from Catholics. There are many different types of Protestant denominations. Today, there are over 2 billion Christians of all denominations worldwide. Of all the major religions, Christianity has the largest number of believers.

Christianity has the largest number of believers.

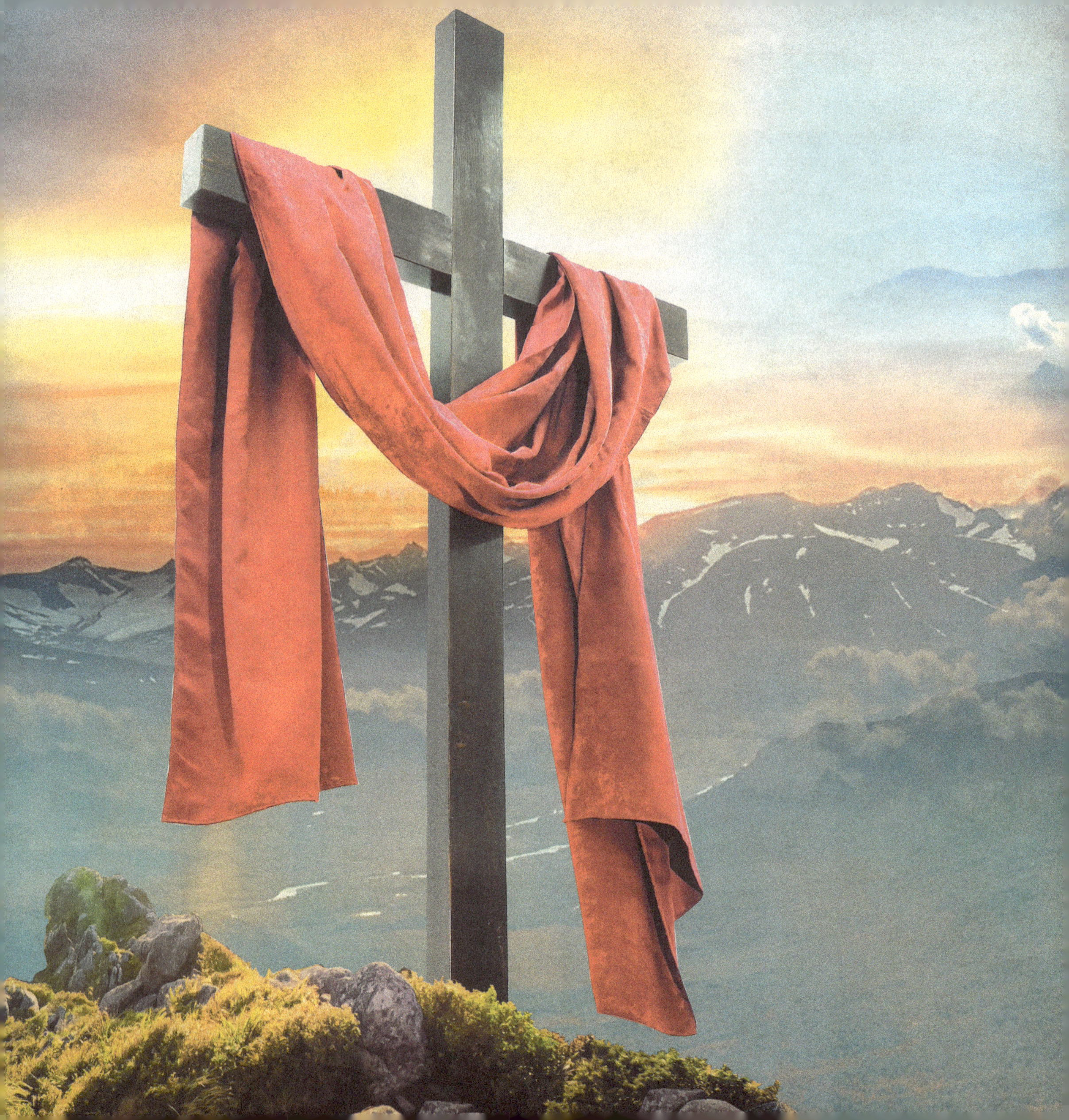

The New Testament

The Bible is made up of the Old and New Testament.

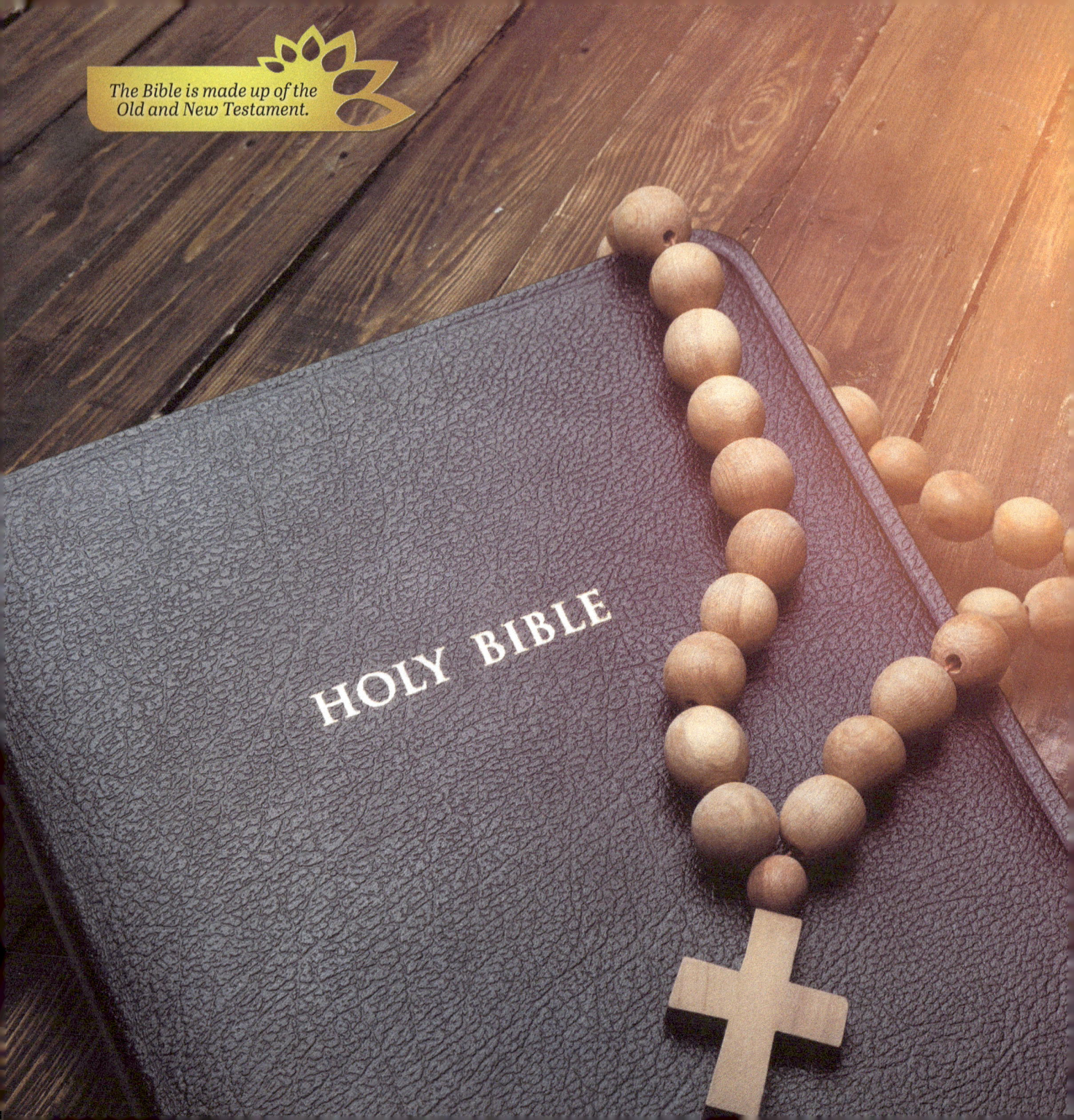

The Bible is made up of two major sections, the Old Testament and the New Testament. The books of the Old Testament were part of the Jewish religion of Judaism.

The New Testament includes gospels written by St. Matthew, St. Mark, St. Luke and St. John. These gospels tell us about the life of Jesus. After the description of his birth and his early life, the gospels describe his miracles and the lessons he taught, often in the form of parables.

St. Matthew, St. Mark, St. Luke and St. John were known as "The Four Evangelists"

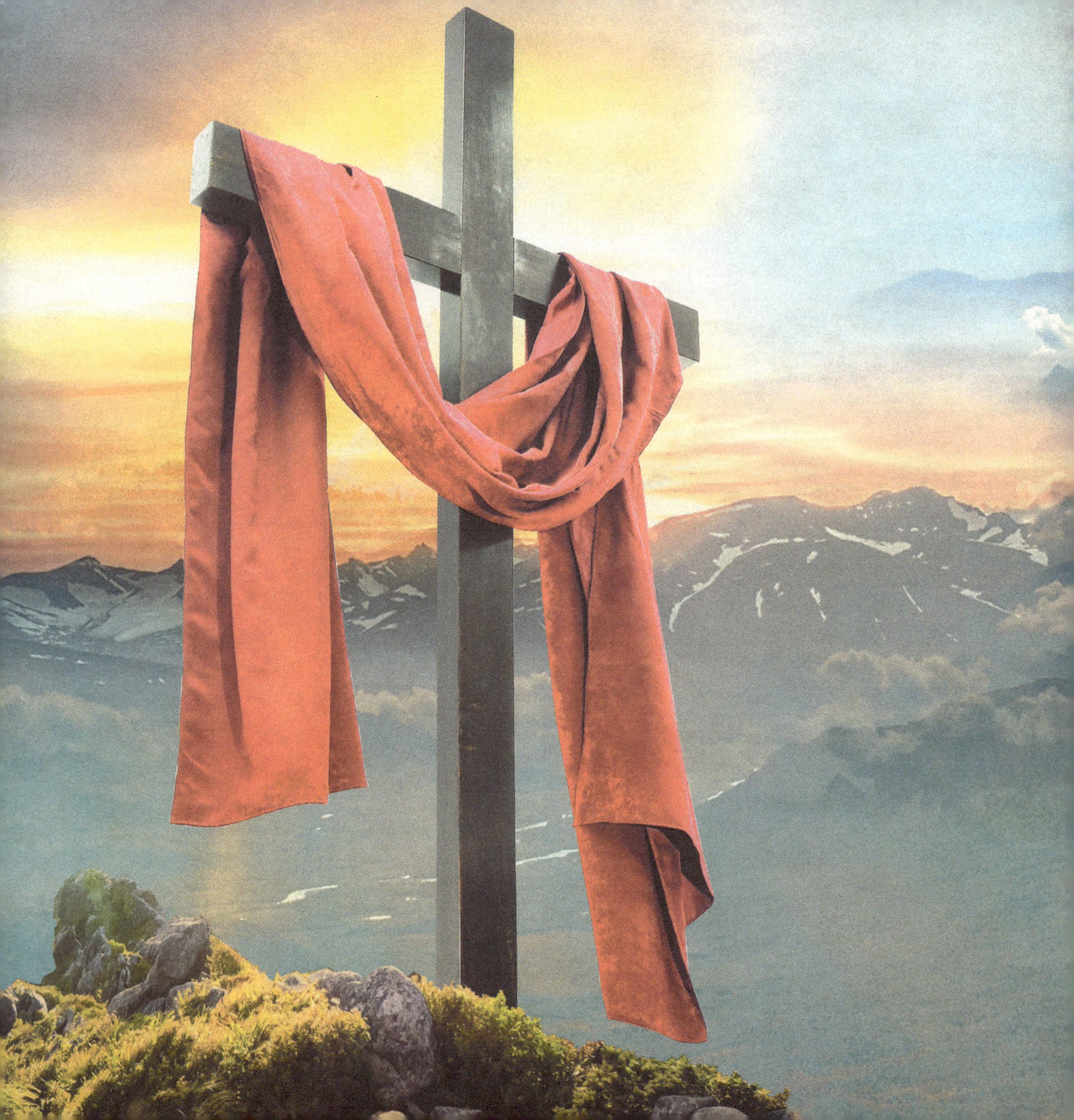

The Early Life of Jesus Christ

An angel came to Joseph and told him to take Mary as his wife.

Jesus Christ was a Jew and was raised by Jewish parents, Joseph and Mary. Joseph and Mary had planned to get married, but then Joseph found out that Mary was already with child. An angel came to Joseph and told him to take Mary as his wife. The angel told him not to fear because Mary was carrying the Son of God. Joseph would be the child's adoptive father.

Bethlehem, Palestine

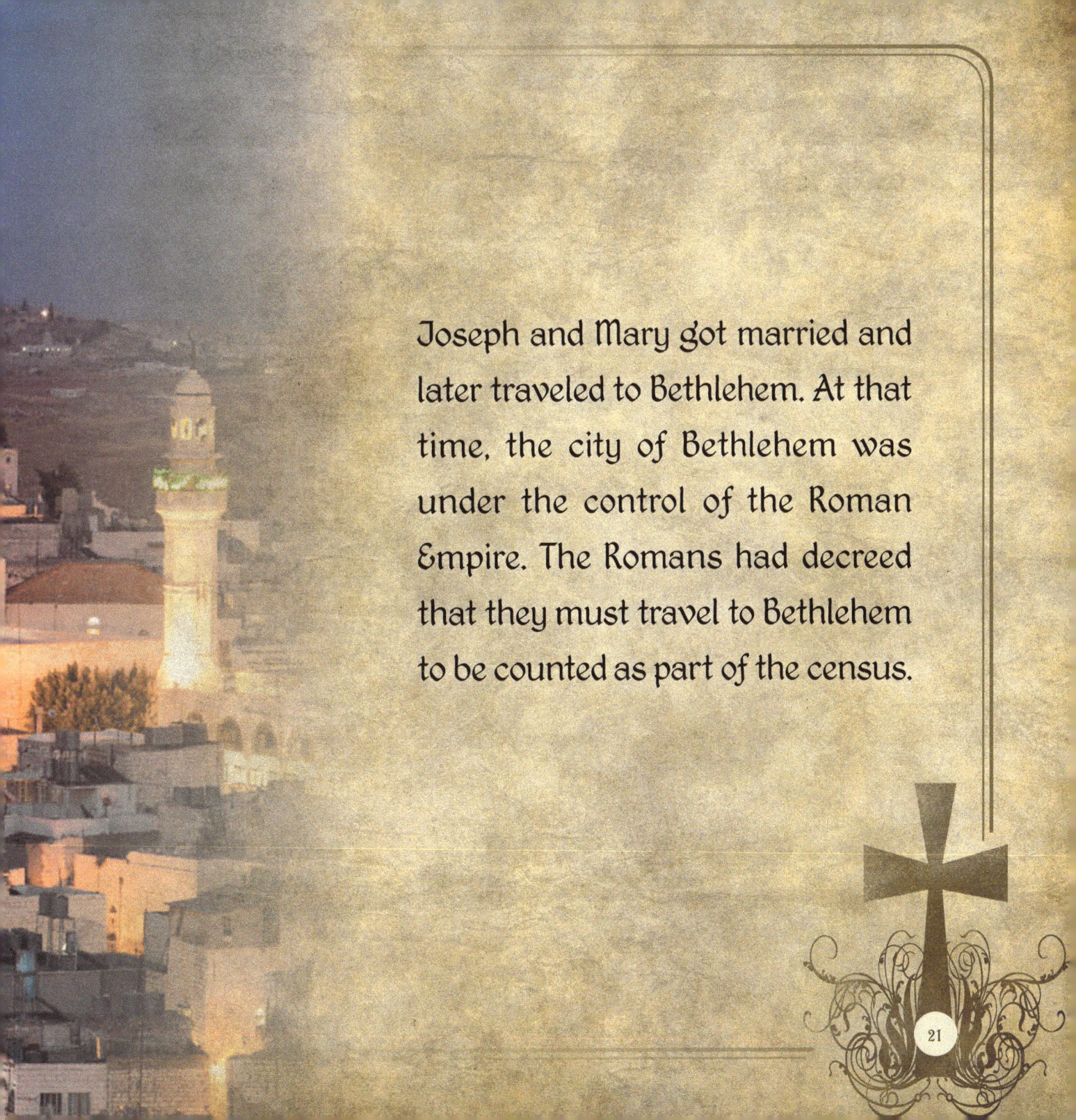

Joseph and Mary got married and later traveled to Bethlehem. At that time, the city of Bethlehem was under the control of the Roman Empire. The Romans had decreed that they must travel to Bethlehem to be counted as part of the census.

Mary was soon to give birth, but they still needed to travel there. Joseph helped Mary get on a donkey's back and he led the donkey as they traveled. However, when they reached their destination, there were no more rooms available.

Joseph and Mary reached Bethlehem but they couldn't find a room to stay in.

Mary placed Jesus in a manger filled with hay so he could sleep.

The keeper of the inn told them that they were welcome to stay in the stable. So, they settled in for the night and that is where Mary gave birth to Jesus. Then, she wrapped Jesus in pieces of cloth. She placed him in a manger filled with hay so he could sleep.

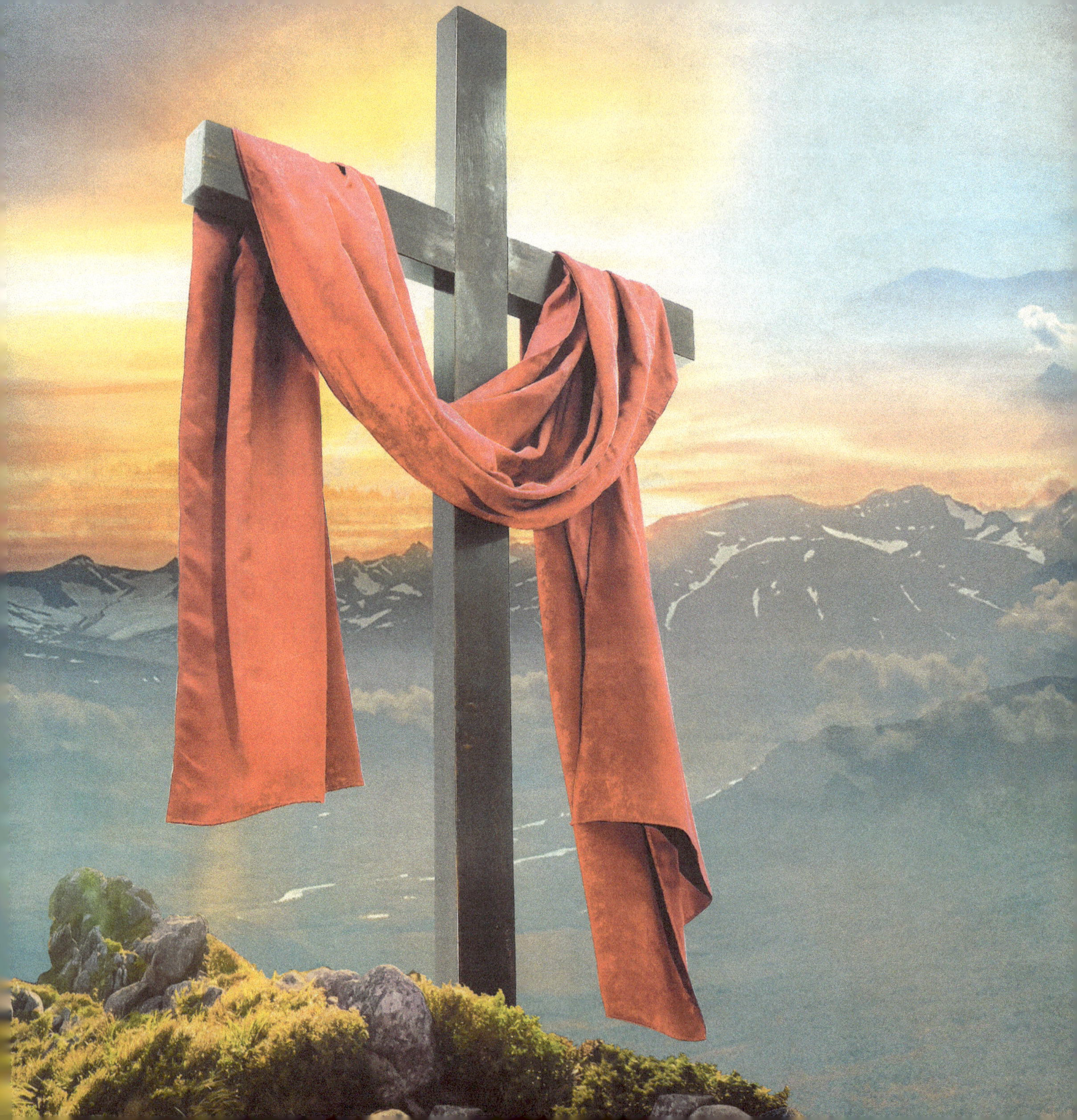

Jesus Went to His Father's House

Joseph, Mary and Jesus

Joseph and Mary brought baby Jesus back to the city of Nazareth where he grew up.

Joseph, Mary and Jesus went on a trip to the city of Jerusalem for Passover.

When he was a young boy, they went on a trip to the city of Jerusalem for Passover, which is a Jewish feast. They went with a huge group of people and sometimes the young children stayed together.

As they traveled back, they realized Jesus was nowhere to be found and they raced back to find him. After three days of looking, they were sick with worry. They finally found him in the temple. He was talking to the priests and wise men and answering their questions. The priests were in awe of his thorough and knowledgeable answers.

Jesus was talking to the priests and wise men and answering their questions.

"Didn't you know that I had to be present at my father's house?" Jesus said to Mary.

When his mother Mary questioned why he had gotten them so worried, he simply said, "Didn't you know that I had to be present at my father's house?" Mary and Joseph didn't fully understand what he meant, but it's clear from this story that he knew he was God's Son.

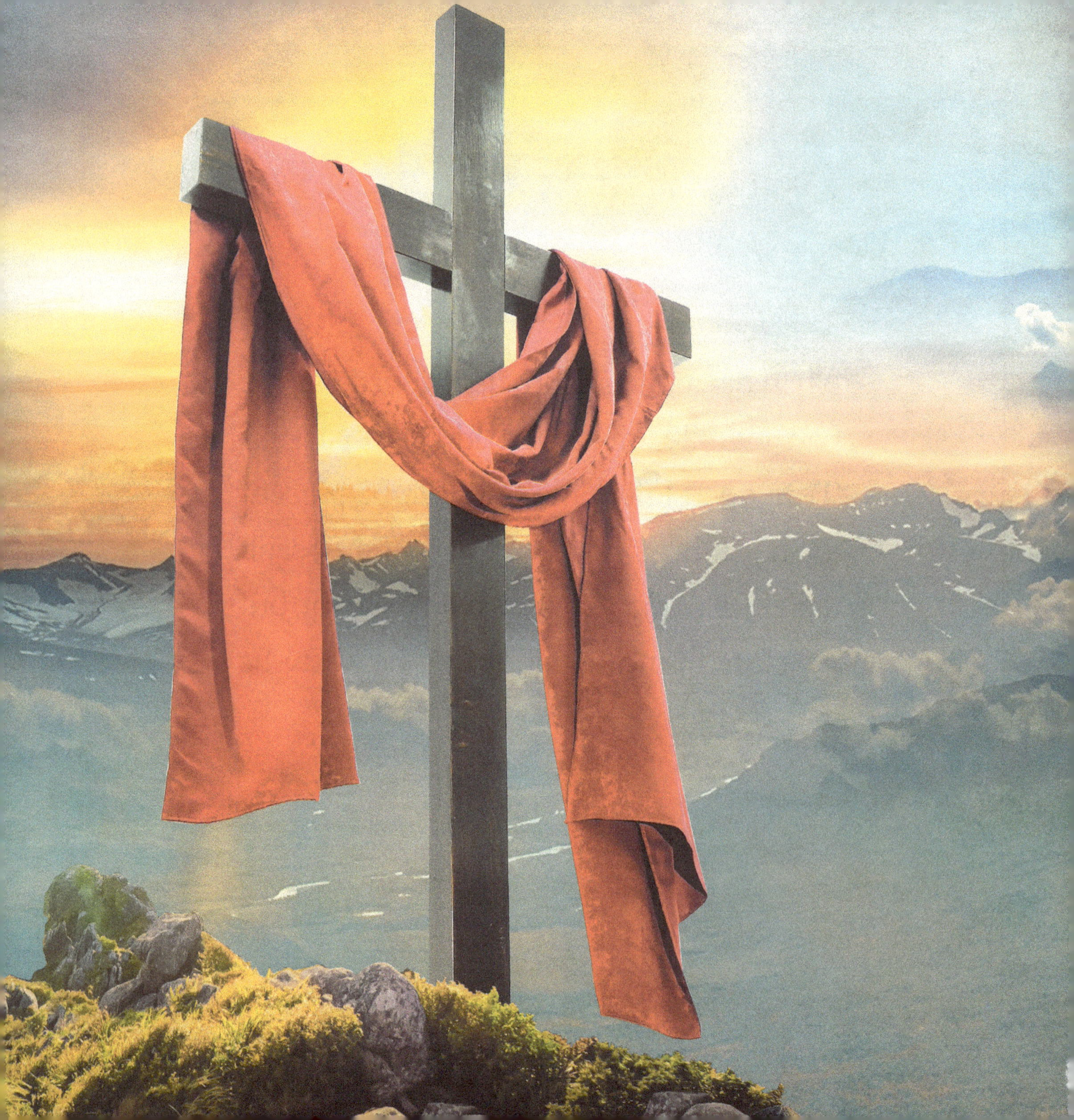

Jesus Performed Miracles

Jesus brought some people back to life after they had died.

Throughout Jesus' life he performed many miracles. He cured the sick including those who had devastating diseases such as leprosy and he gave blind people the ability to see. Even more amazingly, he brought some people back to life after they had died.

He took bread and fishes and multiplied them many times over to feed a crowd of thousands of people. He walked on water. He appeared to his disciples after he had died on the cross and had gone to heaven. Many people witnessed these events.

Jesus walking on water.

For centuries, the Jewish people had been looking for a savior who would be their king. His birth had been predicted in the Old Testament, the Jewish Bible. Many people believed that Jesus was this savior, called the Messiah. The Jews who didn't believe he was the Messiah were disturbed by his presence and the Roman rulers were concerned because many people were following Jesus from place to place to hear him preach the word of God.

Many people believed that Jesus was this savior, called the Messiah.

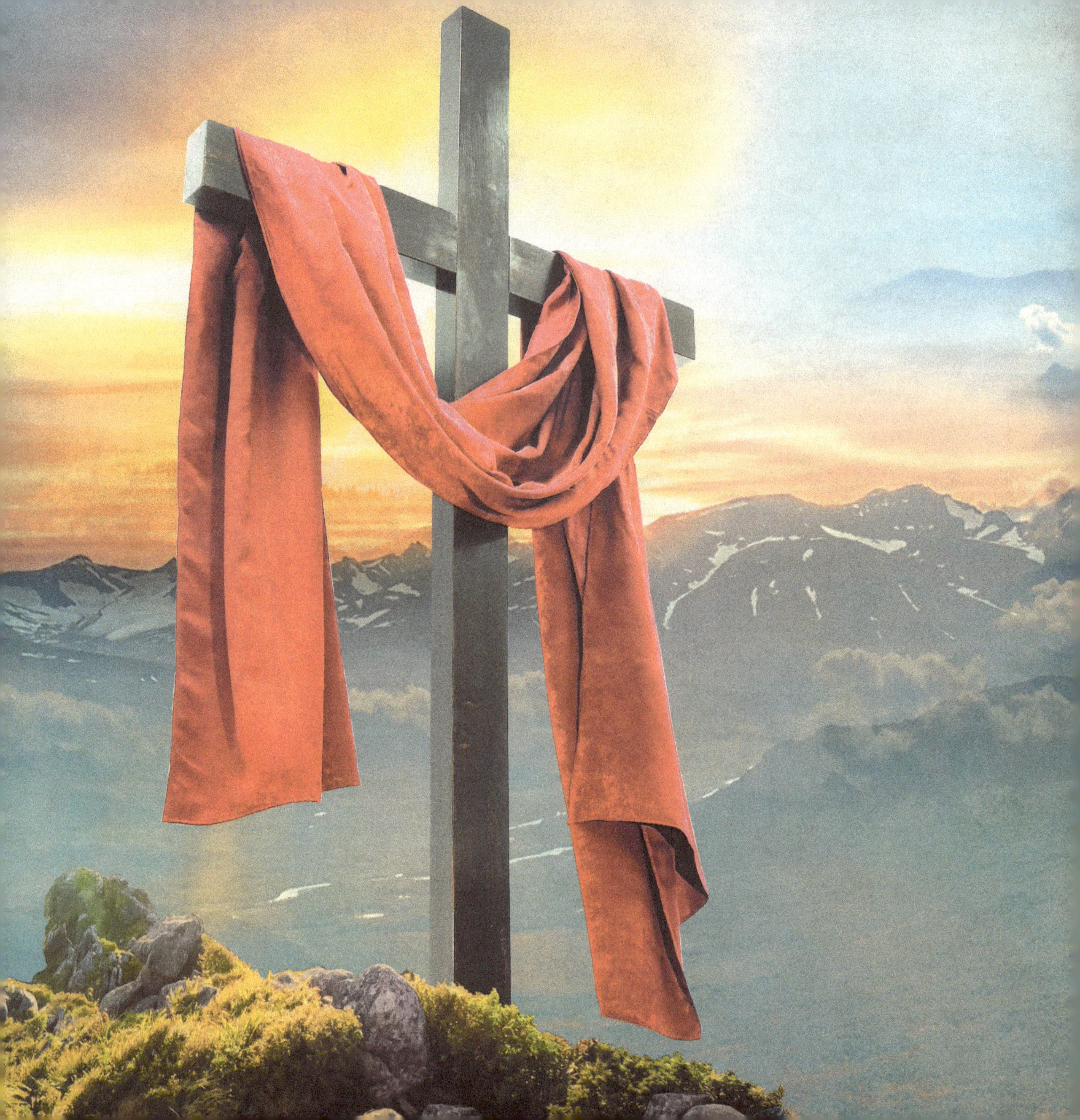

Jesus Taught by Telling Parables

Jesus preaching from a boat on the shore of the Sea of Galilee.

As Jesus' reputation grew, many people came to hear him speak. When he spoke to the crowds, he told them stories in parables. These were simple, heartfelt stories that were designed to explain complicated spiritual ideas or morals. In some cases, the parables he told were easy to understand, but for others it takes contemplation and study to uncover the deep meaning at their core.

There are more than thirty parables in the New Testament and they range in topics from the importance of loving your neighbor to the mysteries of the kingdom of heaven to the understanding that material riches don't bring happiness or grace.

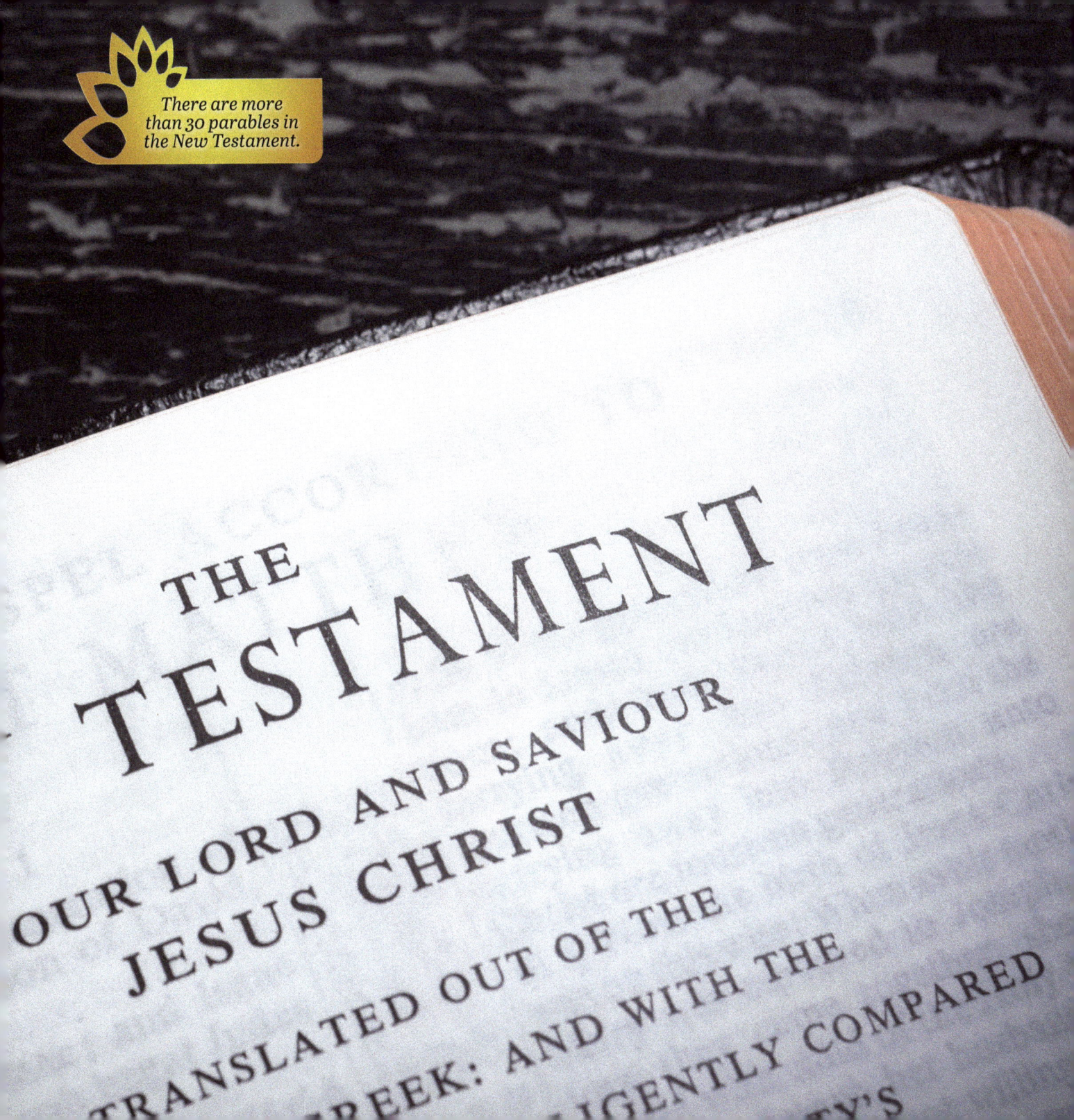

There are more than 30 parables in the New Testament.

THE TESTAMENT

OUR LORD AND SAVIOUR JESUS CHRIST

TRANSLATED OUT OF THE GREEK: AND WITH THE ILIGENTLY COMPARED

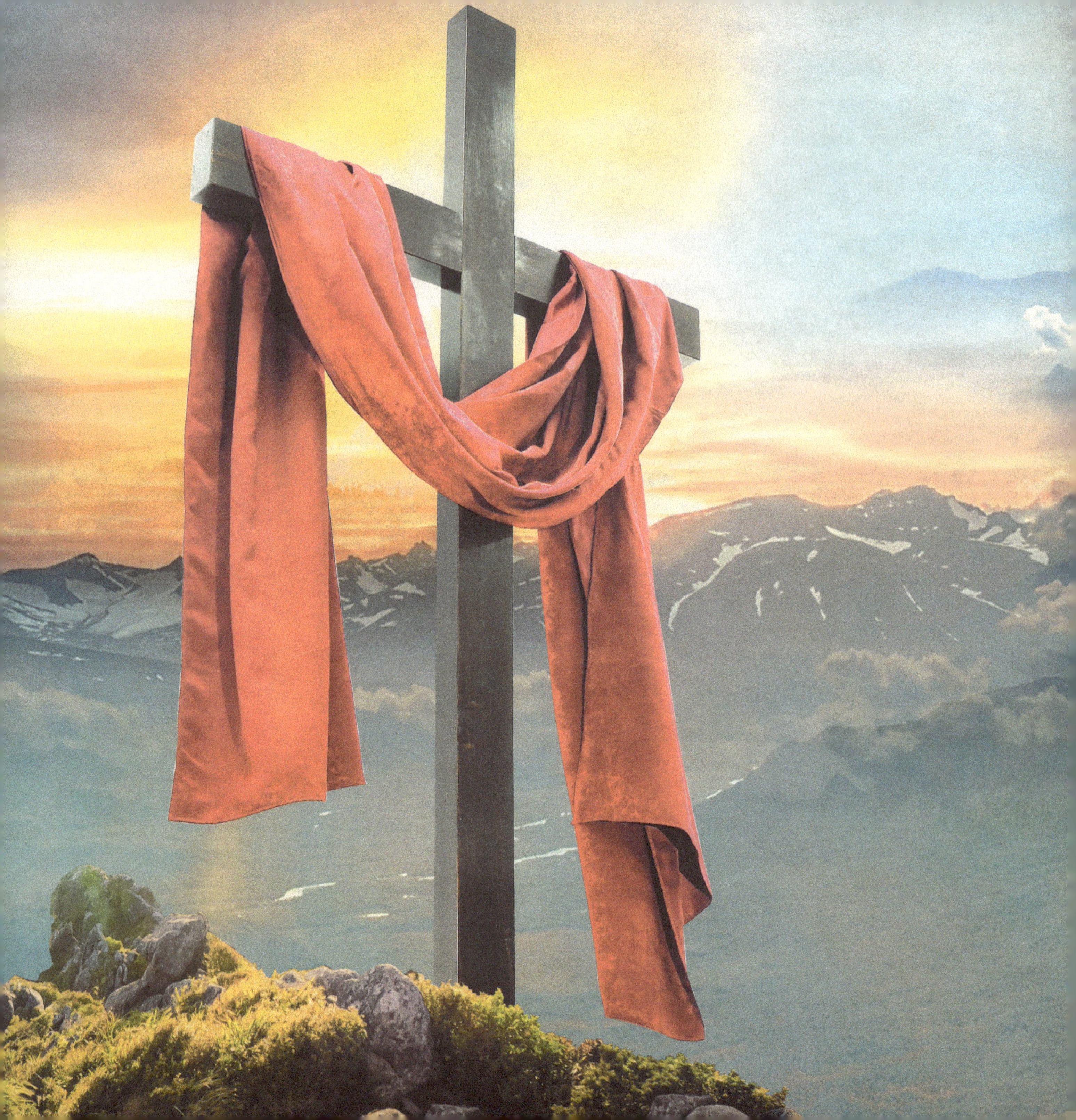

Jesus Dies on the Cross

Historians believe that Jesus taught and performed miracles for about three years. He had twelve apostles who were his followers and traveled with him. Before his death, Jesus gathered the apostles together to have a

Jesus gathered the apostles together to have a Last Supper with them.

Last Supper with them. He shared bread and wine with them and told them that the bread was his body and the wine was his blood. He wanted them to continue to remember him in this way after he left the Earth.

Jesus was betrayed by Judas.

Soon thereafter, Jesus was betrayed by Judas, one of his own apostles. Jesus was brought to the Roman governor, Pontius Pilate.

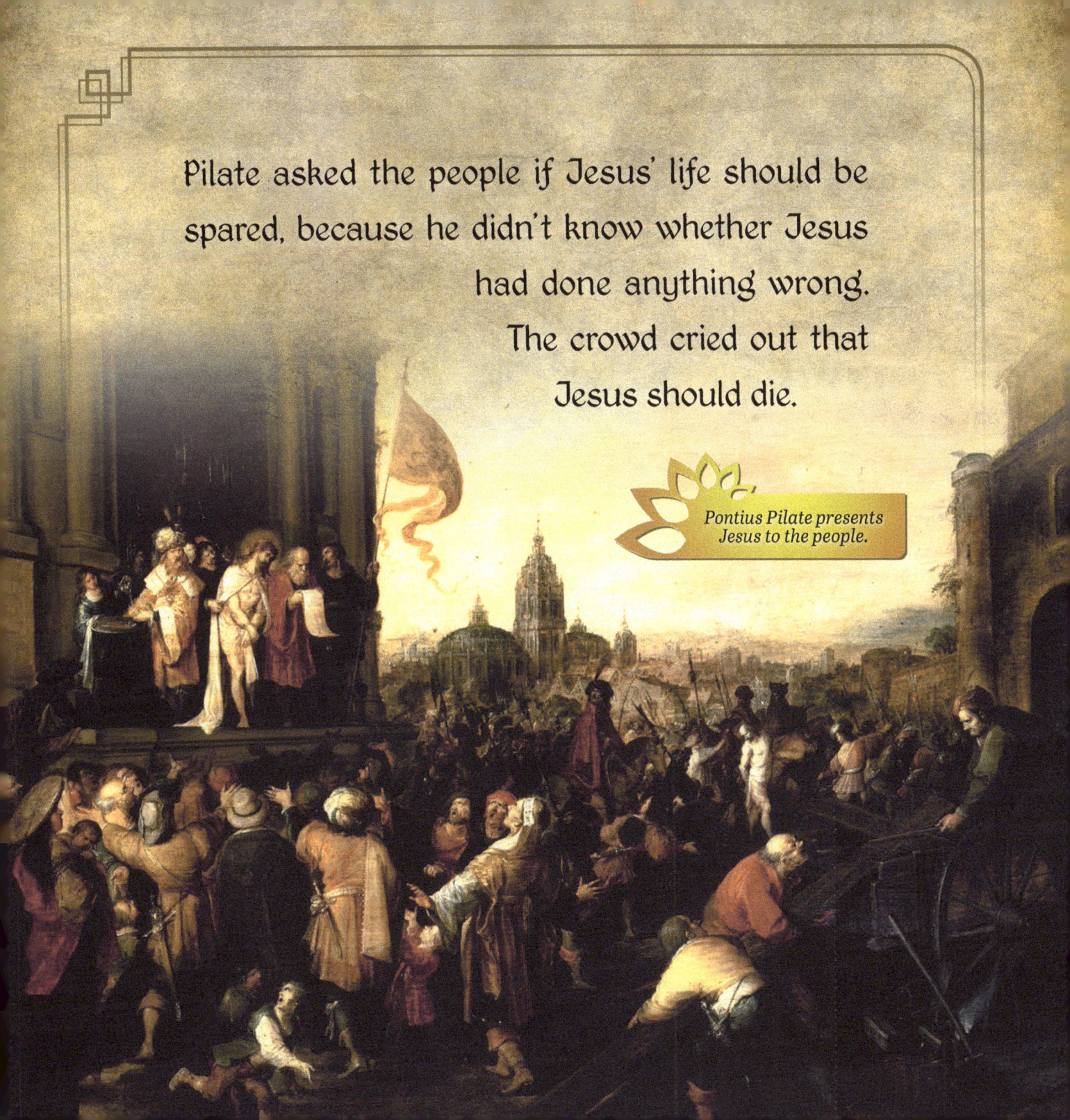

Pilate asked the people if Jesus' life should be spared, because he didn't know whether Jesus had done anything wrong. The crowd cried out that Jesus should die.

Pontius Pilate presents Jesus to the people.

Pontius Pilate had Jesus crucified.

So, Pontius Pilate had Jesus crucified, which means he was hung up on a cross with nails in his hands and feet until he died. But, that wasn't the end, because Jesus appeared to his apostles after he had died. His spirit was on Earth for 40 days as he continued to teach his followers about salvation and the afterlife.

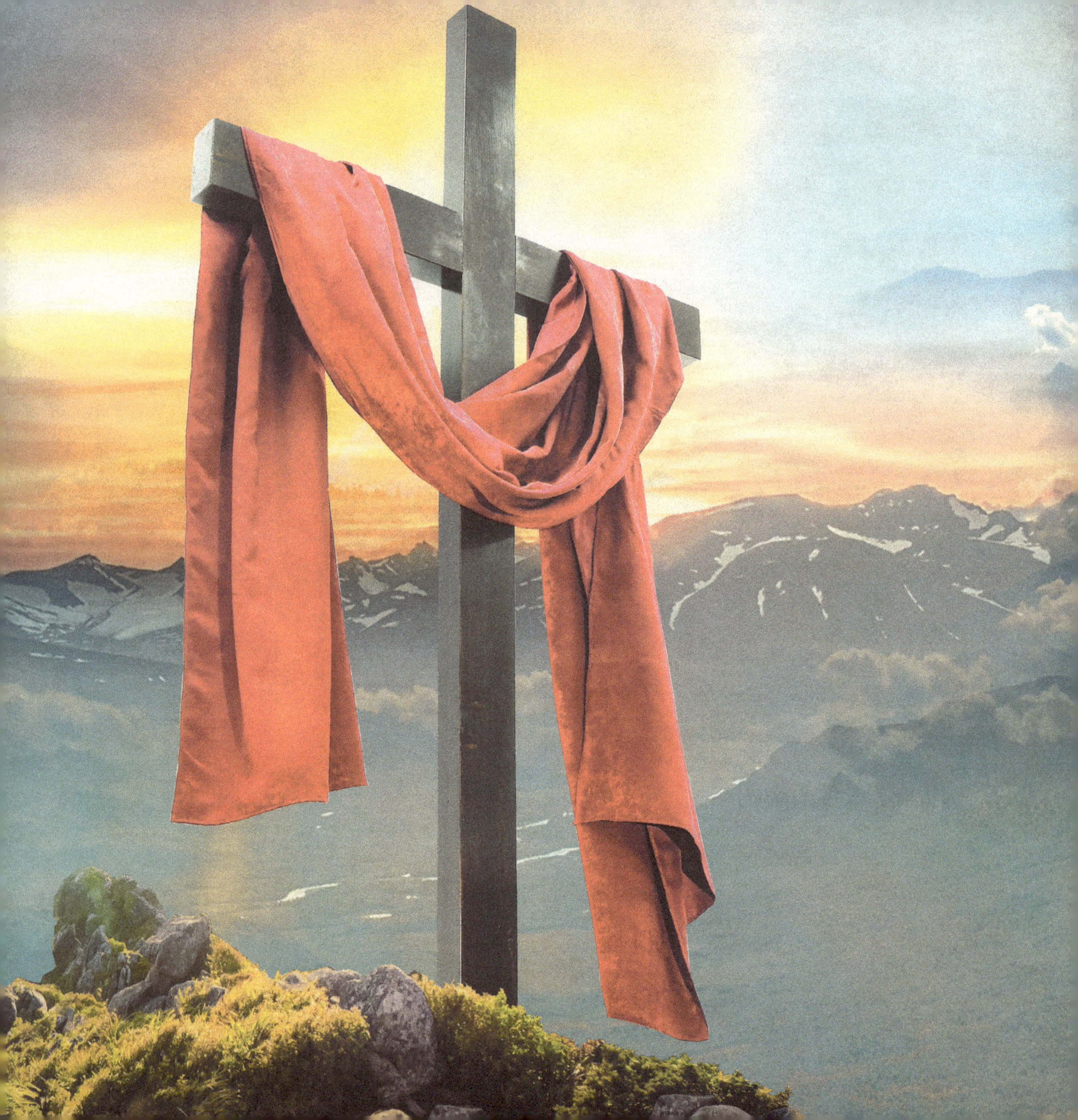

The Apostles Spread the Word

After Jesus was no longer with them, the twelve apostles began to spread the news of his life, death, resurrection, and ascension into heaven. They weren't Jews any longer. Now they were Christians and their religion was Christianity.

The Twelve Apostles

Others persecuted them for their beliefs. One of the men who persecuted Christians in the early days was a man by the name of Saul who was a devout, educated Jew from the country we know as Turkey today. He felt that the beliefs of Christianity were in opposition to his Jewish beliefs and traditions.

Saul of Tarsus, commonly known as Saint Paul

He was on his way to Damascus to seek out Jesus' followers and arrest them. A light came down from heaven upon him and Jesus spoke to Saul. The others who were with him also heard Jesus' voice. Saul was blinded for three days. Then, he converted to Christianity and was eventually known as St. Paul the Apostle. He believed that Jesus was the Son of God and the Messiah even though he had never met Jesus when Jesus was on Earth.

The conversion of Saul.

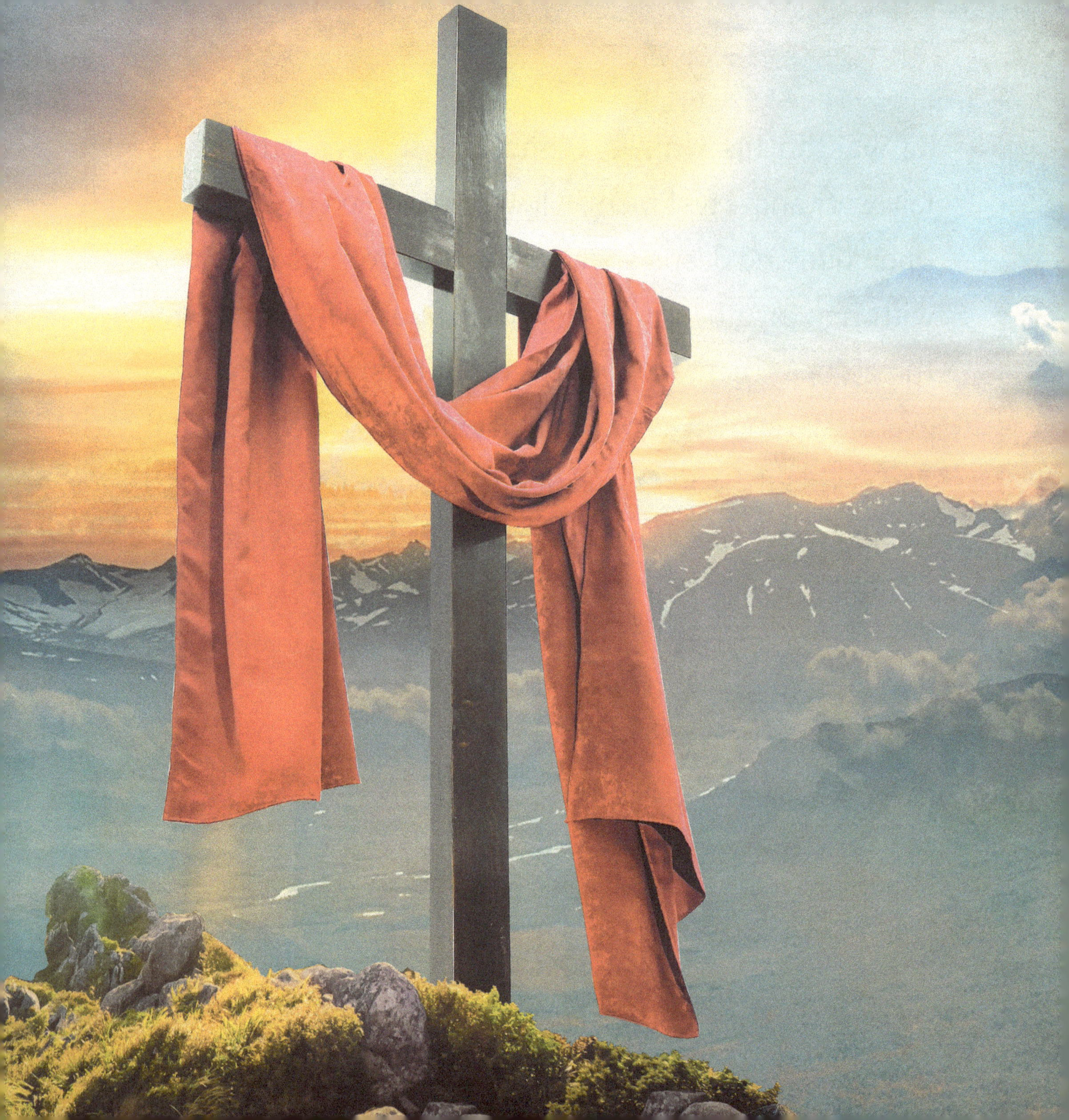

Paul Travels Throughout the Mediterranean

After St. Paul converted to Christianity, he began to preach the word that Jesus Christ was the Messiah. He traveled extensively throughout the Roman Empire in the lands that surrounded the Mediterranean Sea.

St. Paul began to preach the word that Jesus Christ was the Messiah.

St. Paul writing the Epistles.

In addition to preaching in person, he also wrote copious numbers of letters to the first Christian churches and communities. These letters were eventually called Epistles and some of them became part of the New Testament.

St. Paul became the first missionary and unlike the other apostles who had preached only to Jewish people, Paul preached to people who weren't Jewish.

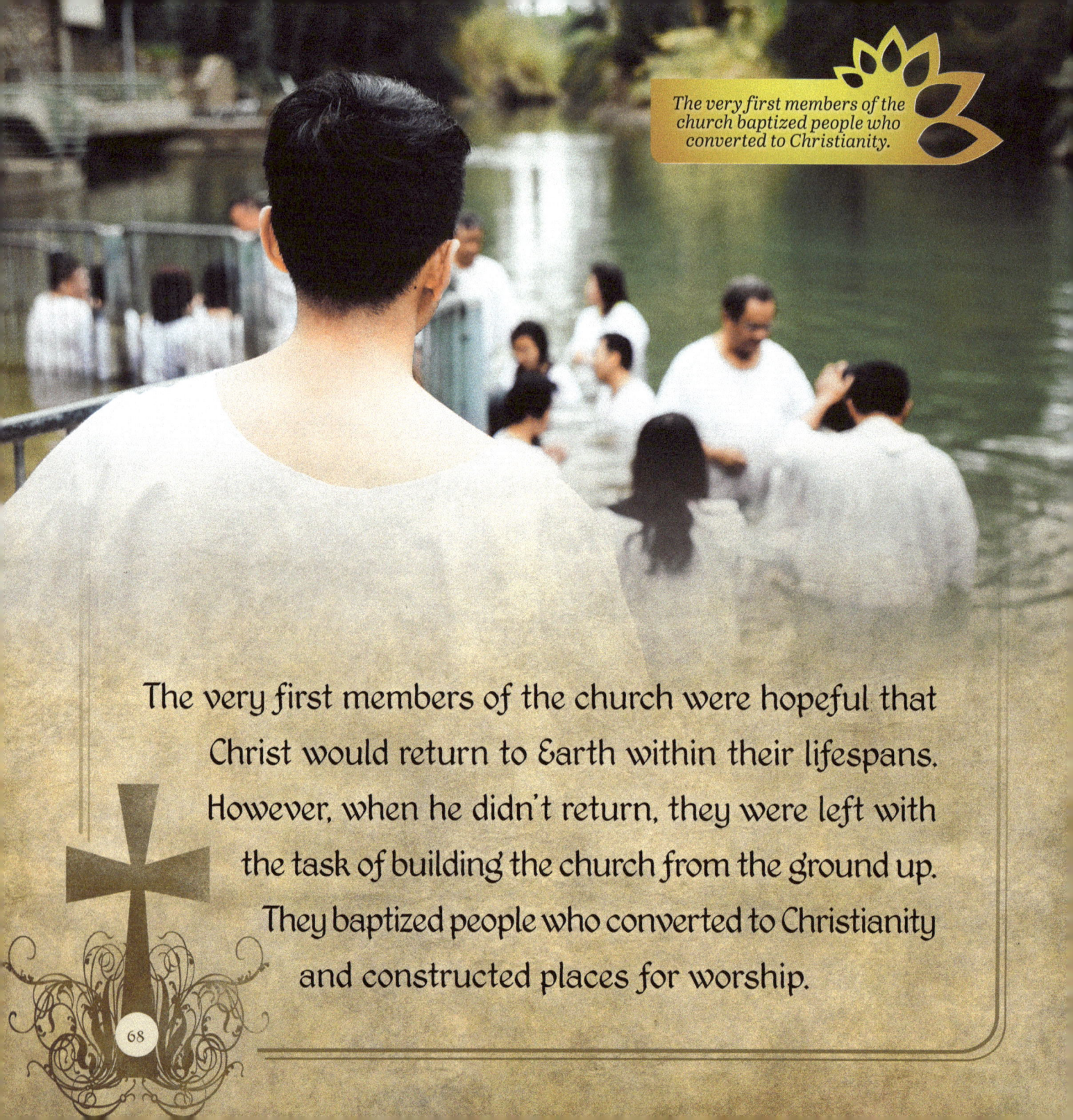

The very first members of the church baptized people who converted to Christianity.

The very first members of the church were hopeful that Christ would return to Earth within their lifespans. However, when he didn't return, they were left with the task of building the church from the ground up. They baptized people who converted to Christianity and constructed places for worship.

St. Peter

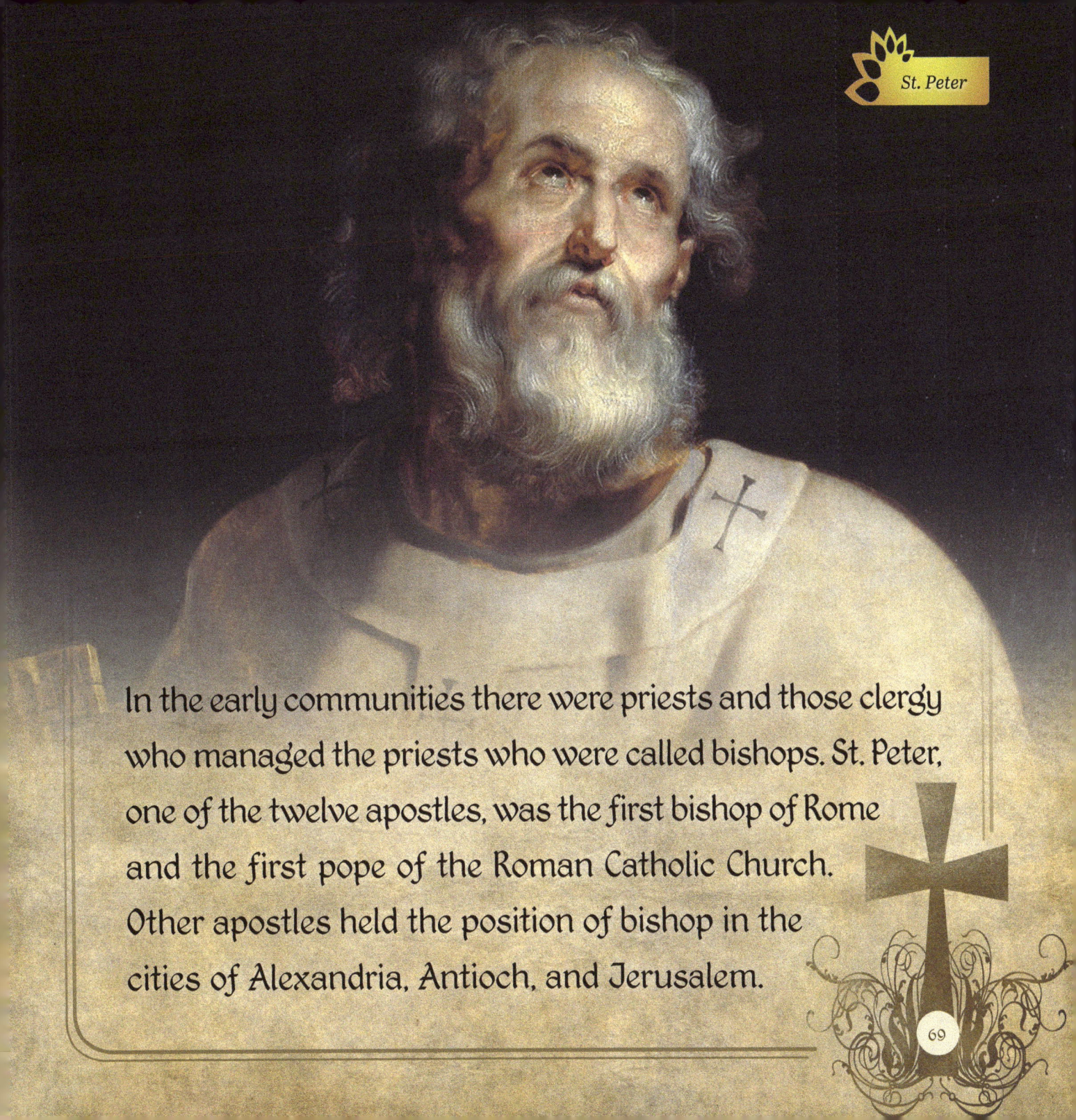

In the early communities there were priests and those clergy who managed the priests who were called bishops. St. Peter, one of the twelve apostles, was the first bishop of Rome and the first pope of the Roman Catholic Church. Other apostles held the position of bishop in the cities of Alexandria, Antioch, and Jerusalem.

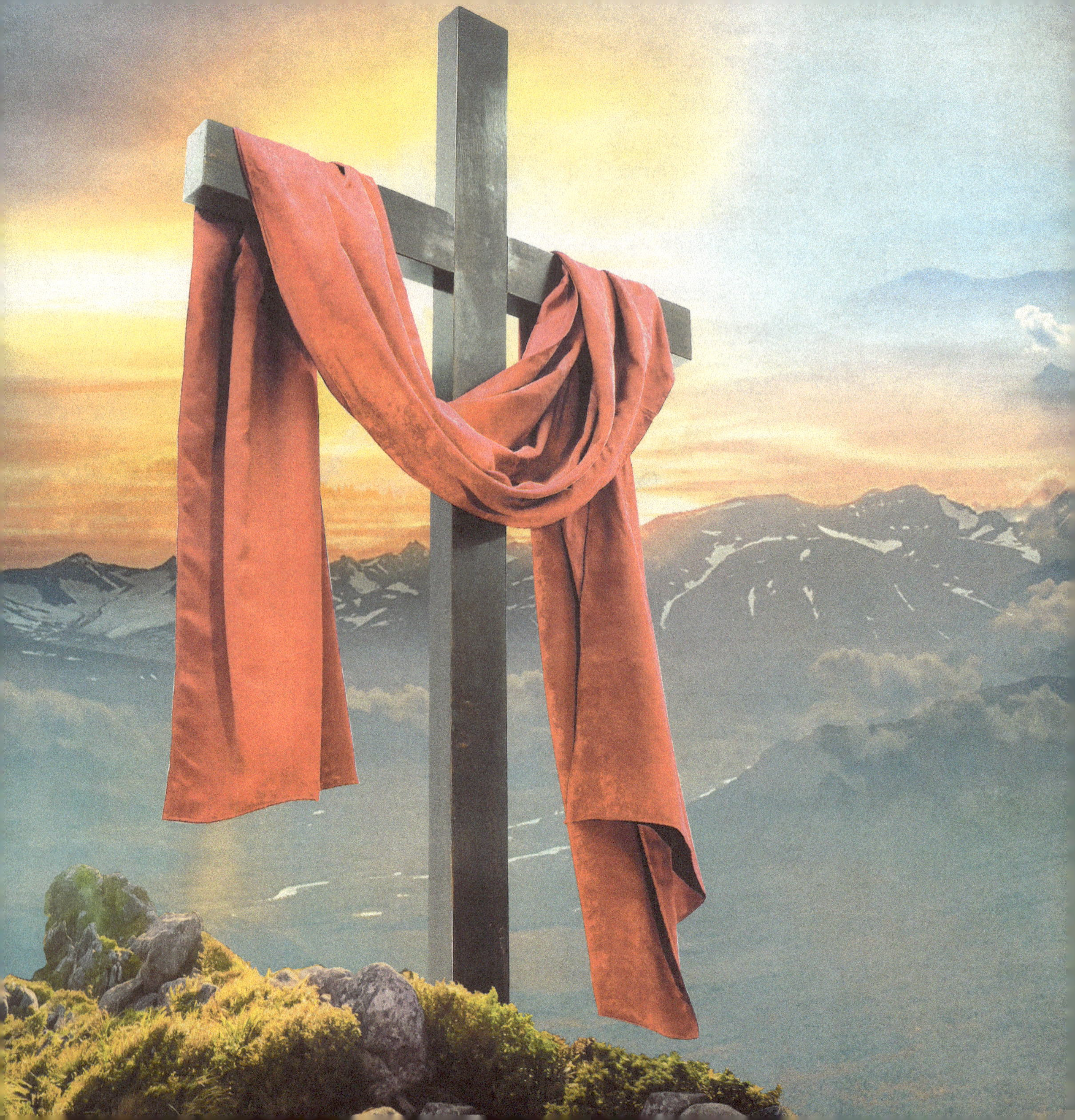

The Romans Persecuted the Christians

Nero and the Great Fire of Rome, 64 AD

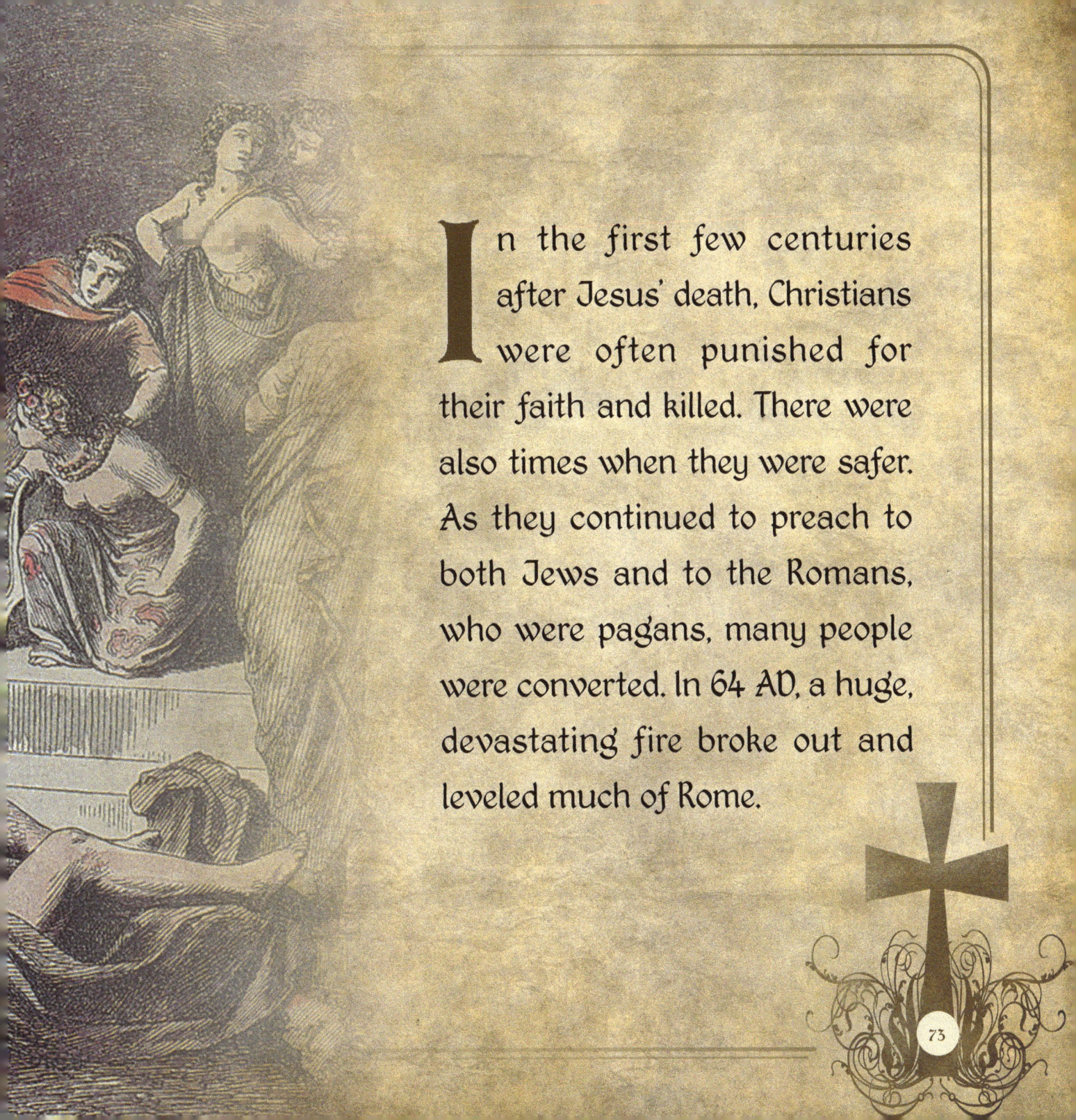

In the first few centuries after Jesus' death, Christians were often punished for their faith and killed. There were also times when they were safer. As they continued to preach to both Jews and to the Romans, who were pagans, many people were converted. In 64 AD, a huge, devastating fire broke out and leveled much of Rome.

The people believed that Nero, their emperor, had started the fire. To deflect attention from his guilt, Nero ordered that Christians be rounded up and put to death. They were tortured, torn apart by wild dogs or burned alive.

Throughout the next centuries, Christians were persecuted and died as martyrs for their faith. But, eventually Christianity would prevail over paganism. In 323 AD, Christianity became the official religion of the Roman Empire.

Nero burning Christians as torches.

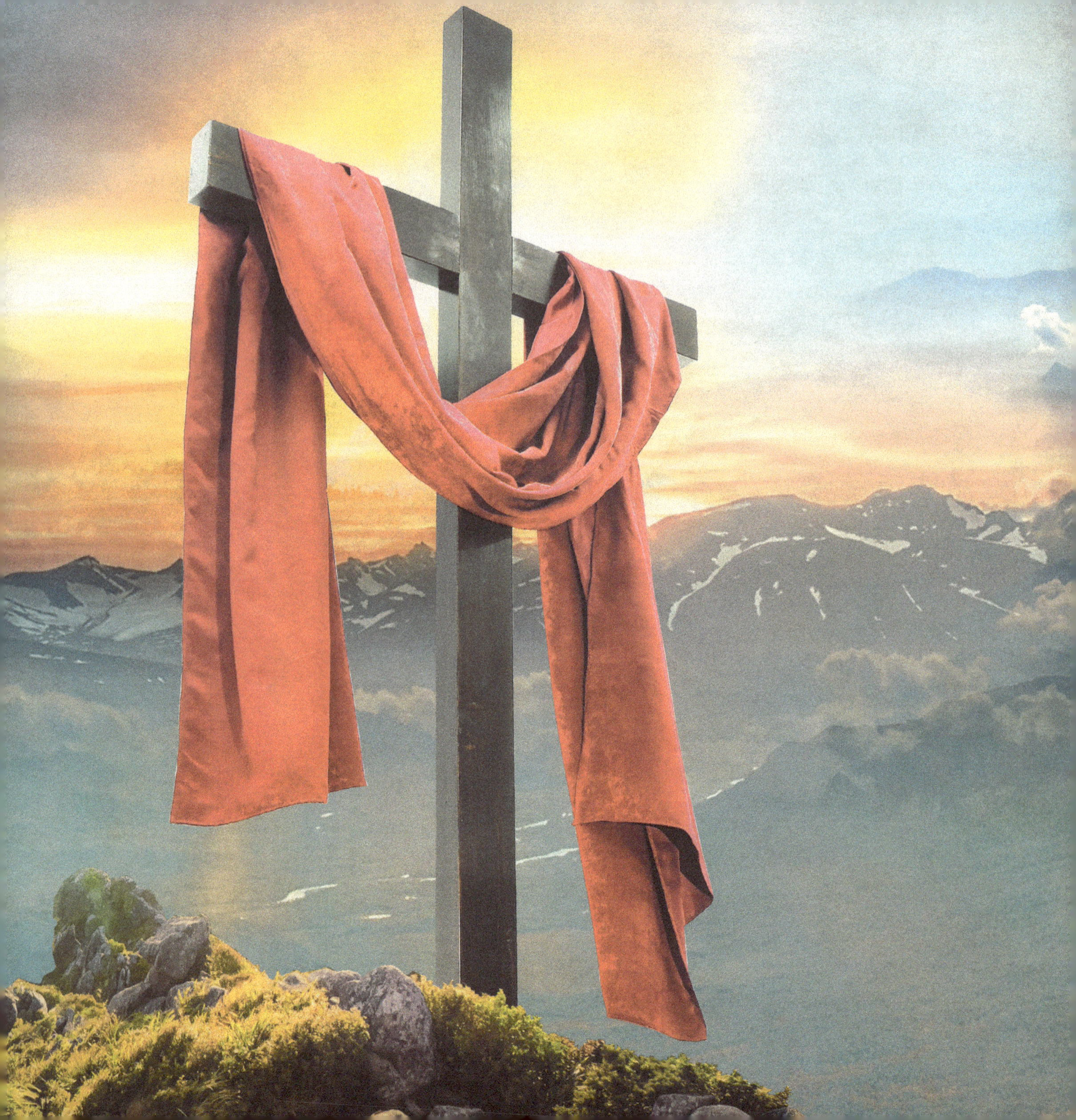

Summary

Over 2,000 years ago, Jesus was born in a stable in Bethlehem. In the Old Testament, the Jewish Bible, there had been many references to the birth of a savior, called the Messiah. This savior would die for the sins of humanity. During his lifetime, Jesus performed many miracles and taught using simple stories with complex meanings called parables. As he preached and taught, many people came to believe that he was the Son of God and the Messiah.

After he died on a cross, his apostles saw him before he ascended into heaven. They thought he would come back to Earth again soon. When he did not come back, the apostles and other Christians began to build a church. St. Paul who was a converted Jew began to spread the beliefs of Christianity throughout the Roman Empire. The Romans were pagans and believed in many different gods, but eventually they were converted to Christianity. Today, Christianity is the religion with the largest number of followers worldwide, over 2 billion.

Awesome! Now that you've learned about the beginnings of Christianity, you may want to read some Bible stories about Jesus in the Baby Professor book, *The Storybook of Jesus – Short Stories from the Bible | Children & Teens Christian Books.*

Visit
www.SpeedyBookStore.com

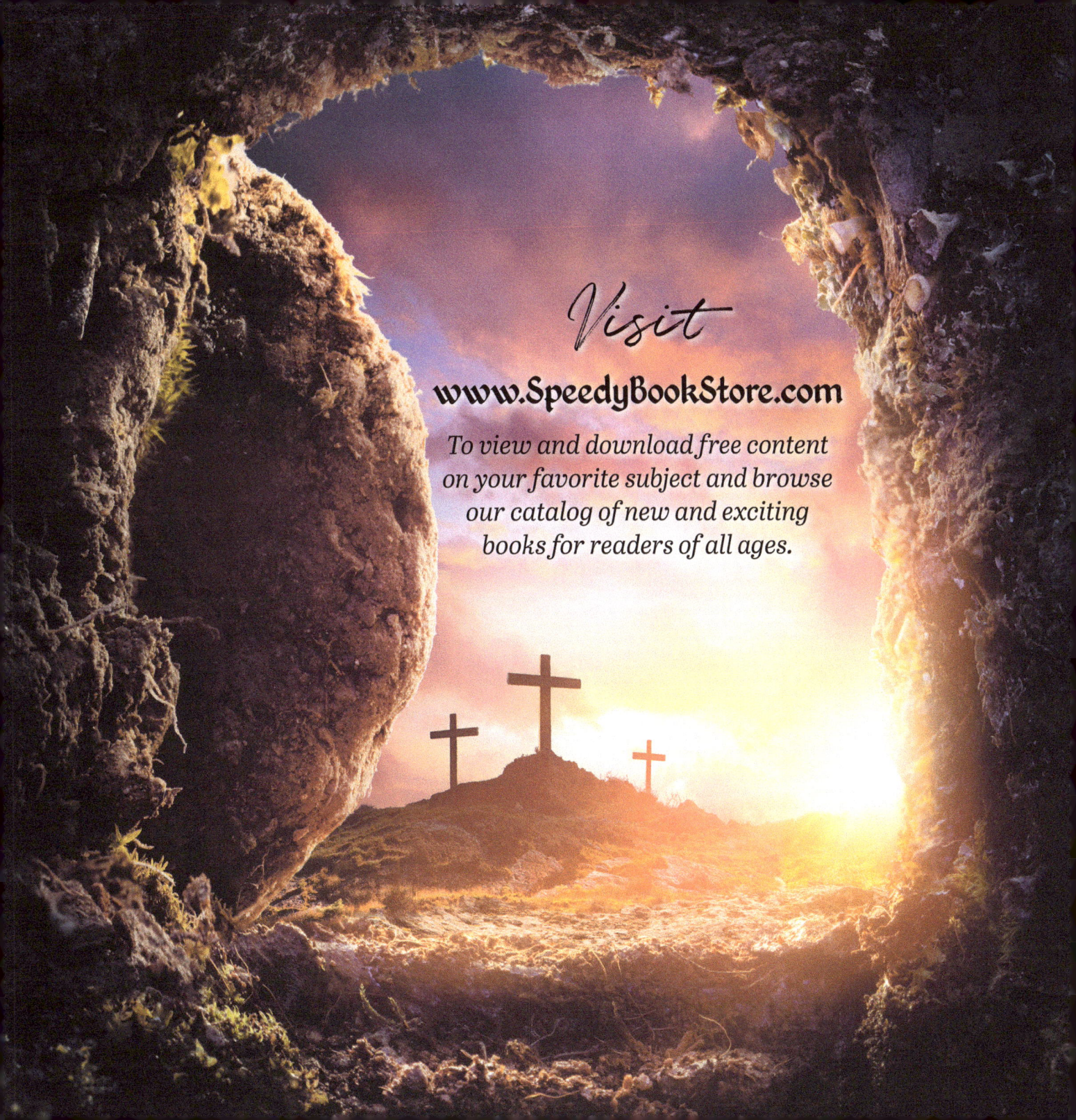

To view and download free content on your favorite subject and browse our catalog of new and exciting books for readers of all ages.